Excellent!

©Disney

Perfect work!

©Disney

GW00732847

©Disney

Brilliant!

©Disney

I love to read!

©Disney

Let's practise!

©Disney

Well done!

©Disney

You deserve a reward!

©Disney

Excellent!

©Disney

Reading is fun!

©Disney

Well done!

©Disney

A great effort!

©Disney

Good work!

©Disney

I love to read!

©Disney

Word perfect!

©Disney

You deserve a reward!

©Disney

Great reading!

©Disney

Good effort!

©Disney

STEPS TO READING

Dear Parent:

Congratulations! Your child is taking the first steps on an exciting journey. **The destination? Independent reading!**

STEPS TO READING will help your child get there. The programme offers three steps to reading success. Each step includes fun stories and colourful art, and the result is a complete literacy programme with something for every child.

Learning to Read, Step by Step!

(1) **Start to Read   Nursery – Preschool**
• **big type and easy words** • **rhyme and rhythm** • **picture clues**
For children who know the alphabet and are eager to begin reading.

(2) **Let's read together   Preschool – Year 1**
• **basic vocabulary** • **short sentences** • **simple stories**
For children who recognise familiar words and sound out new words with help.

(3) **I can read by myself   Years 1-3**
• **engaging characters** • **easy-to-follow plots** • **popular topics**
For children who are ready to read on their own.

STEPS TO READING is designed to give every child a successful reading experience. The year levels are only guides. Children can progress through the steps at their own speed, developing confidence in their reading, no matter what their year.

Remember, a lifetime love of reading starts with a single step!

This edition published by Parragon in 2011

Parragon
Queen Street House
4 Queen Street
Bath BA1 1HE, UK

Copyright © 2011 Disney Enterprises, Inc.
Based on the "Winnie the Pooh" works by
A. A. Milne and E. H. Shepard.

ISBN 978-1-4454-2116-2

Printed in Malaysia

Disney

Winnie the Pooh

Pooh's Easter Egg Hunt

Bath • New York • Singapore • Hong Kong • Cologne • Delhi
Melbourne • Amsterdam • Johannesburg • Auckland • Shenzhen

"Happy Easter!"
Winnie the Pooh
called to his friends.

It was time for
the Easter egg hunt.

Rabbit said,
"Whoever finds
the most eggs wins.
Get ready,
get set . . . go!"

Pooh, Piglet,
Roo, Eeyore
and Kanga walked
into the woods.

Pooh found a yellow egg

under some daffodils.

He put the egg

in his basket.

But Pooh did not know

his basket had a hole.

The egg fell out

onto the grass.

Piglet found
Pooh's yellow egg.
"Lucky me!" he said.

Then Pooh found

a purple egg

behind a rock.

That egg slipped out, too!

Roo found Pooh's egg.
"Oh, goody!" he cried.
"Purple is my
favourite colour!"

Pooh found a green egg
and put it in his basket.
But he did not
see it fall out.

Tigger found
Pooh's green egg.
"I am on my way
to winning!" he said.

Pooh found a red egg.
It fell through the hole,
too.

Eeyore found
Pooh's red egg.
"Oh, my," he said.
"I found one."

On the side of a hill,
Pooh found a blue egg.
"How pretty!" he said.

Pooh walked up the hill-
but the blue egg rolled
down the hill!

Kanga found
Pooh's blue egg
next to a log.

"Time is up!"
Rabbit shouted.
Everyone ran over
to see who had won.

Pooh's friends
each showed their
Easter eggs.

Pooh looked inside
his empty basket.
"My eggs seem to be
hiding again," he said.

Piglet looked at the basket.
He poked his hand
through the hole.
"I think I know why,"
said Piglet.

"You can have my
yellow egg," said Piglet.
"It was probably your egg
before it was mine."

"Thank you, Piglet,"
said Pooh.
"And you can have my
purple egg," said Roo.

"Here, Buddy Bear,"
said Tigger.
"Tiggers like to win
fair and square."

Eeyore gave Pooh
his red egg.
"It was too good
to be true," said Eeyore.
Kanga said,
"Take mine, Pooh!"

Rabbit counted the eggs.

"Pooh is the winner!"
he cried.

"You win an Easter feast."

"Is there enough food
for everyone?"
asked Pooh.

"I can make more,"
said Rabbit.

"Is there enough honey?" asked Pooh.

"Of course!" said Rabbit.

"Hooray!" said Pooh.

The feast was great fun.

Everyone ate Easter eggs!

But Pooh liked

the honey best!

Now turn
over for the
next story...

By Isabel Gaines
Illustrated by Josie Yee

DISNEP

Winnie the Pooh

Pooh's Halloween Pumpkin

PaRRagon

Bath · New York · Singapore · Hong Kong · Cologne · Delhi
Melbourne · Amsterdam · Johannesburg · Auckland · Shenzhen

One spring day,
Christopher Robin
and Pooh saw
Rabbit planting seeds.

"What are
you planting?"
asked Pooh.
"Pumpkin seeds,"
said Rabbit.

"I want to
grow a pumpkin,
too," said Pooh.
"Growing a pumpkin
is hard work,"
said Rabbit.

"I will take
good care of it,"
promised Pooh.
So Rabbit gave
him a seed.

Christopher Robin
and Pooh
planted the seed
in a sunny spot.

"I will watch
the pumpkin
grow," said Pooh.

"But the pumpkin
will not be ready
until the fall,"
said Christopher Robin.
"I will wait,"
said Pooh.

"First I need
something to eat,"
said Pooh.
So Pooh went home.
He took all his
honey outside.

Pooh watched the spot
where the seed
was planted.
Pooh ate and watched
and ate some more.

Soon it was summer.
Piglet came along.
"What a pretty vine
you are growing, Pooh!"
said Piglet.

"But I wanted
a pumpkin,
not a vine,"
said Pooh.

Pooh watched the vine.

He ate some honey.

Pooh ate and watched

and ate some more.

Soon the vine grew

a flower.

"I wanted a pumpkin,
not a flower!"
Pooh told Owl.
"Maybe you are not
growing a pumpkin,"
said Owl.

"You have a vine.

You have a flower.

I think you are

growing . . ."

". . . a cucumber!"

said Owl.

"Do cucumbers
taste good
with honey?"
asked Pooh.

Pooh scratched
his head.
"A pumpkin seed
should grow into
a pumpkin," he said.

So Pooh watched
the plant.

He watered it.

He ate more honey.

One day, Pooh woke
from a nap.
The air was cooler.
The leaves were
changing colours.

"There is a green
ball on your vine,"
said Eeyore.
"But I wanted a
pumpkin!" said Pooh.

"Oh, well,"
said Eeyore.
"I never get
what I want, either."

Weeks passed.

The green ball

grew bigger.

And so did

Pooh's tummy!

One day, part of
the ball turned
orange.

Soon all of the
ball was orange.
Leaves fell from
the trees.
There was a big
orange pumpkin
on Pooh's vine!

Everyone gathered
around Pooh's
pumpkin.

"The pumpkin looks
like your tummy!"
said Tigger.
"You grew with
the pumpkin!"
said Christopher Robin.

The friends decided
to carve the pumpkin
for Halloween.

"I will carve the eyes,"
said Owl.

"I will carve the nose,"
said Rabbit.

"And I will carve
the mouth,"
said Piglet.

Pooh's Halloween
pumpkin made
the best
jack-o'-lantern in
the Hundred-Acre Wood.